I Can Say No

Tracy Mcneil

This Book Belongs To

_____

BAD TOUCH

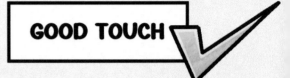

GOOD TOUCH

About The Author

TRACY MCNEIL IS AN AUTHOR DEDICATED TO
EMPOWERING YOUNG CHILDREN AND TEACHING
THEM VALUES FROM AN EARLY AGE. AS A WIFE, MOTHER,
GRANDMOTHER, AND MINISTER, SHE BRINGS A WEALTH
OF PERSONAL EXPERIENCE TO HER WRITING.
HER WORK IS AIMED AT INSTILLING
RIGHTEOUSNESS AND IMPORTANT VALUES IN CHILDREN.
IN ADDITION TO HER WRITING, MCNEIL IS A SERIAL
ENTREPRENEUR AND SERVES AS A BOARD MEMBER
FOR THE LIBRARY BOARD IN LEWISVILLE, TEXAS,
REFLECTING HER COMMITMENT TO COMMUNITY
SERVICE AND EDUCATION.

Made in the USA
Columbia, SC
31 October 2024

44901981R00018